HOW TO INVEST IN THE STOCK MARKET

How to Invest in the Stock Market

Walter the Educator

Silent King Books
A WhichHead Entertainment Imprint

Copyright © 2024 by Walter the Educator

All rights reserved. No part of this book may be reproduced in any manner whatsoever without written permission except in the case of brief quotations embodied in critical articles and reviews.

First Printing, 2024

Disclaimer

The author and publisher offer this information without warranties expressed or implied. No matter the grounds, neither the author nor the publisher will be accountable for any losses, injuries, or other damages caused by the reader's use of this book. Your use of this book acknowledges an understanding and acceptance of this disclaimer.

How to Invest in the Stock Market is a little problem solver book by Walter the Educator that belongs to the Little Problem Solver Books Series.
Collect them all and more books at WaltertheEducator.com

LITTLE PROBLEM
SOLVER BOOKS

INTRO

Investing in the stock market can be one of the most effective ways to build wealth over time, but it can also be intimidating for beginners. The world of stocks is often portrayed as complex, risky, and exclusive, but in reality, it is accessible to anyone with a basic understanding of financial principles and a willingness to learn. This little book will provide an in-depth guide to investing in the stock market, covering everything from the basics of stocks to advanced strategies and risk management techniques. By the end, you'll have a solid foundation to start investing wisely.

How to Invest in the Stock Market

1. Understanding the Stock Market

Before you can begin investing, it's essential to understand what the stock market is and how it operates. The stock market is essentially a marketplace where investors can buy and sell shares of publicly traded companies. These shares represent partial ownership in a company. When you purchase a stock, you become a shareholder, which gives you a claim to a portion of the company's assets and earnings.

How to Invest in the Stock Market

1.1 Stock Exchanges

Stock exchanges are the platforms where stocks are bought and sold. The most famous exchanges are the New York Stock Exchange (NYSE) and the NASDAQ. Stocks are listed on these exchanges, and their prices are determined by supply and demand. Investors and traders buy and sell shares through brokerage firms that act as intermediaries.

How to Invest in the Stock Market

1.2 Types of Stocks

Stocks can generally be categorized into two main types: common stocks and preferred stocks.

How to Invest in the Stock Market

- **Common Stocks**: These are the most typical type of stock that investors purchase. Common stockholders have voting rights in the company and may receive dividends, although these are not guaranteed. The value of common stocks can fluctuate widely based on the company's performance and broader market conditions.

How to Invest in the Stock Market

- **Preferred Stocks**: These stocks give investors a higher claim to dividends and assets in case the company goes bankrupt. However, preferred stockholders typically do not have voting rights. Preferred stocks are often seen as a hybrid between stocks and bonds.

How to Invest in the Stock Market

1.3 Why Companies Issue Stocks

Companies issue stocks as a way to raise capital for expansion, research, or paying off debts. By selling shares of ownership, a company can fund its operations without having to take out loans. In exchange for purchasing shares, investors hope to benefit from the company's growth through rising stock prices and potential dividends.

How to Invest in the Stock Market

2. How to Start Investing in the Stock Market

If you're new to investing, the process of getting started can seem overwhelming. However, by breaking it down into steps, you can begin to invest confidently.

How to Invest in the Stock Market

2.1 Define Your Financial Goals

The first step to investing is understanding your financial goals. What are you saving for? Is it retirement, buying a home, or building an emergency fund? The clearer your goals, the easier it will be to choose the right investments.

How to Invest in the Stock Market

Your goals will also determine your investment horizon, which is the length of time you plan to keep your money invested. Long-term goals like retirement might allow you to invest more aggressively in stocks, while short-term goals like saving for a car may require a more conservative approach.

How to Invest in the Stock Market

2.2 Educate Yourself

Education is key to successful investing. While you don't need to become a financial expert overnight, understanding basic concepts such as diversification, risk tolerance, and market cycles will help you make informed decisions. Books, financial news, online courses, and podcasts can be valuable resources.

How to Invest in the Stock Market

2.3 Choose a Brokerage Account

To start buying stocks, you need to open a brokerage account. A brokerage acts as a middleman between you and the stock market. Many online brokerages offer platforms that allow you to buy and sell stocks with low fees. When choosing a brokerage, consider factors like ease of use, customer service, research tools, and commission costs.

How to Invest in the Stock Market

Some popular brokerage platforms include:

- **Fidelity**: Known for its research tools and wide range of investment options.
- **Charles Schwab**: Offers low-cost trades and a user-friendly platform.
- **Robinhood**: Known for commission-free trades and a mobile-friendly interface.

How to Invest in the Stock Market

2.4 Understand Different Types of Accounts

When you open a brokerage account, you'll typically have a few options regarding the type of account. The two main types are taxable brokerage accounts and tax-advantaged accounts like Individual Retirement Accounts (IRAs).

How to Invest in the Stock Market

- **Taxable Brokerage Account**: This is a standard account that allows you to buy and sell stocks freely. However, you'll be taxed on any capital gains or dividends.

How to Invest in the Stock Market

- **Tax-Advantaged Accounts (IRA or Roth IRA)**: These accounts offer tax benefits for long-term investing, particularly for retirement. The main difference between a traditional IRA and a Roth IRA is when you pay taxes. In a traditional IRA, contributions may be tax-deductible, but you'll pay taxes on withdrawals in retirement. With a Roth IRA, you contribute after-tax dollars but can withdraw tax-free in retirement.

How to Invest in the Stock Market

3. Fundamental Concepts in Stock Market Investing

Once you've opened a brokerage account and are ready to start investing, it's important to familiarize yourself with key investment concepts that can help guide your decisions.

How to Invest in the Stock Market

3.1 Risk Tolerance

Risk tolerance is the degree of variability in investment returns that an investor is willing to withstand. It's influenced by factors like your financial situation, investment timeline, and personal comfort with fluctuations in the market. Investors with a high-risk tolerance may be more willing to invest in volatile stocks with the potential for higher returns, while those with a lower risk tolerance might prefer stable investments, such as bonds.

How to Invest in the Stock Market

3.2 Diversification

Diversification is a risk management strategy that involves spreading your investments across different types of assets, industries, or geographical regions. By diversifying, you reduce the risk of a single investment negatively impacting your entire portfolio. For example, if you invest all your money in one company and that company underperforms, you could lose a significant portion of your investment. However, if you spread your investments across several companies, industries, or asset classes (like stocks, bonds, and real estate), the risk is mitigated.

How to Invest in the Stock Market

3.3 Dollar-Cost Averaging

Dollar-cost averaging is an investment strategy where you consistently invest a fixed amount of money at regular intervals, regardless of market conditions. This method reduces the impact of market volatility, as it spreads your investments over time. When prices are high, your fixed investment amount will buy fewer shares, and when prices are low, you'll be able to buy more shares. Over the long term, this strategy can help smooth out market fluctuations and reduce the emotional impact of investing during turbulent times.

How to Invest in the Stock Market

4. Types of Investments in the Stock Market

There are several types of investments you can make in the stock market, depending on your goals, risk tolerance, and financial situation.

How to Invest in the Stock Market

4.1 Individual Stocks

Investing in individual stocks allows you to buy shares of specific companies. This approach gives you control over your investments but also comes with higher risk. The value of a stock can fluctuate significantly based on the performance of the company, market conditions, and economic factors.

How to Invest in the Stock Market

4.2 Exchange-Traded Funds (ETFs)

ETFs are a popular investment vehicle for beginners because they offer instant diversification. When you buy shares of an ETF, you are investing in a portfolio of stocks or other assets that track an index, sector, or specific investment theme. For example, an ETF might track the performance of the S&P 500, a broad market index that includes 500 of the largest U.S. companies.

How to Invest in the Stock Market

ETFs are generally considered lower risk than individual stocks because they spread your investment across many companies, reducing the impact of any single company's performance.

How to Invest in the Stock Market

4.3 Mutual Funds

Mutual funds pool money from multiple investors to buy a diversified portfolio of stocks, bonds, or other assets. Unlike ETFs, mutual funds are actively managed by professional fund managers who aim to outperform the market. However, mutual funds often come with higher fees due to the active management involved.

How to Invest in the Stock Market

4.4 Bonds

Bonds are fixed-income securities that represent a loan made by an investor to a borrower (usually a corporation or government). Bonds are typically considered safer investments than stocks, but they offer lower potential returns. Investors often use bonds to balance out the risk in their portfolios.

How to Invest in the Stock Market

5. Building a Stock Portfolio

Once you've understood the different types of investments available, the next step is to start building your portfolio.

How to Invest in the Stock Market

5.1 Asset Allocation

Asset allocation refers to how you divide your investments among different asset classes, such as stocks, bonds, and cash. The right asset allocation depends on your risk tolerance and investment horizon. Generally, younger investors with a longer time horizon can afford to take on more risk and invest heavily in stocks, while older investors nearing retirement may prefer a more conservative allocation with a higher percentage of bonds.

How to Invest in the Stock Market

A common rule of thumb is to subtract your age from 100 to determine the percentage of your portfolio that should be invested in stocks. For example, if you're 30 years old, you might consider allocating 70% of your portfolio to stocks and 30% to bonds. However, this is just a general guideline, and your actual allocation should be based on your individual circumstances.

How to Invest in the Stock Market

5.2 Rebalancing Your Portfolio

Over time, the value of your investments will fluctuate, which can cause your asset allocation to become unbalanced. For example, if your stocks perform well, they might start to make up a larger percentage of your portfolio than you originally intended. Rebalancing involves selling some assets and buying others to bring your portfolio back to your target allocation. It's important to periodically review and rebalance your portfolio to maintain the right balance of risk and return.

How to Invest in the Stock Market

6. Advanced Strategies for Stock Market Investing

As you gain more experience in the stock market, you may want to explore more advanced investment strategies. These strategies involve a deeper understanding of market trends, financial analysis, and timing.

How to Invest in the Stock Market

6.1 Fundamental Analysis

Fundamental analysis involves evaluating a company's financial health and intrinsic value based on factors like earnings, revenue, profit margins, and debt levels. Investors who use fundamental analysis believe that a stock's price will eventually reflect its true value, and they seek to buy undervalued stocks and hold them until the market corrects itself.

How to Invest in the Stock Market

6.2 Technical Analysis

Technical analysis is the study of historical price movements and trading volumes to predict future price trends. This strategy focuses on charts, patterns, and market indicators to identify short-term buying and selling opportunities. Technical analysis is often used by traders who aim to profit from short-term price fluctuations rather than long-term growth.

How to Invest in the Stock Market

6.3 Dividend Investing

Dividend investing focuses on buying stocks that pay regular dividends, which are a portion of a company's profits distributed to shareholders. Dividend-paying stocks can provide a steady income stream and are often seen as less risky than growth stocks. Investors who prioritize income may build a portfolio of high-quality dividend-paying stocks and reinvest their dividends to compound returns over time.

How to Invest in the Stock Market

7. Managing Risk in the Stock Market

While the stock market has the potential to generate substantial returns, it also comes with risks. Proper risk management is essential to protect your investment capital and achieve long-term success.

How to Invest in the Stock Market

7.1 Know Your Risk Tolerance

Understanding your risk tolerance is crucial to making investment decisions that align with your comfort level. If you're uncomfortable with the idea of losing a significant portion of your investment during a market downturn, you may want to consider a more conservative investment approach.

How to Invest in the Stock Market

7.2 Emergency Fund

Before investing, it's wise to establish an emergency fund that can cover 3 to 6 months' worth of living expenses. This fund acts as a safety net in case of unexpected financial challenges, such as a job loss or medical emergency. By having an emergency fund in place, you can avoid selling your investments during a downturn to cover expenses.

How to Invest in the Stock Market

7.3 Avoid Emotional Investing

One of the biggest mistakes investors make is allowing emotions to drive their decisions. Fear and greed can lead to impulsive actions, such as selling in a panic during a market crash or chasing after hot stocks in a booming market. Successful investors remain disciplined, stick to their long-term strategies, and avoid reacting to short-term market noise.

How to Invest in the Stock Market

7.4 Avoid Timing the Market

Many investors are tempted to time the market by predicting when prices will rise or fall. However, this approach is notoriously difficult, even for professional investors. Attempting to time the market can result in missed opportunities or buying at the wrong time. Instead, focus on a long-term strategy that aligns with your financial goals and risk tolerance.

How to Invest in the Stock Market

8. The Power of Compounding

One of the greatest advantages of investing in the stock market is the power of compounding. Compounding occurs when your investment gains generate additional gains over time. For example, if you invest $1,000 and earn a 10% return, you'll have $1,100 at the end of the first year. In the second year, you'll earn a 10% return on the $1,100, not just the original $1,000. Over time, this compounding effect can lead to exponential growth in your investment portfolio.

How to Invest in the Stock Market

OUTRO

Investing in the stock market is a powerful way to build wealth and achieve long-term financial goals. While it can be intimidating for beginners, with the right knowledge and strategies, anyone can become a successful investor. Start by defining your financial goals, understanding your risk tolerance, and choosing the right investment vehicles, whether individual stocks, ETFs, or mutual funds. Diversify your portfolio, avoid emotional investing, and take advantage of the power of compounding to grow your wealth over time.

By remaining disciplined, patient, and informed, you can navigate the stock market's ups and downs and achieve financial success.

ABOUT THE CREATOR

Walter the Educator is one of the pseudonyms for Walter Anderson. Formally educated in Chemistry, Business, and Education, he is an educator, an author, a diverse entrepreneur, and he is the son of a disabled war veteran.
"Walter the Educator" shares his time between educating and creating. He holds interests and owns several creative projects that entertain, enlighten, enhance, and educate, hoping to inspire and motivate you. Follow, find new works, and stay up to date with Walter the Educator™
at WaltertheEducator.com

www.ingramcontent.com/pod-product-compliance
Lightning Source LLC
LaVergne TN
LVHW010437070526
838199LV00066B/6060